JUMP STARTS FOR CATECHISTS

Reflections
on the Catechism

Twenty-Third Publications
A Division of Bayard
One Montauk Avenue, Suite 200
New London, CT 06320
(860) 437-3012 or (800) 321-0411
www.23rdpublications.com

The Scripture passages contained herein are from the *New Revised Standard Version of the Bible*, Catholic edition, copyright © 1989, 1993, Division of Christian Education of the National Council of Churches in the U.S.A. Used by permission; all rights reserved.

ISBN-10: 1-58595-598-1
ISBN 978-1-58595-598-5
Printed in the U.S.A.

Jump Starts FOR CATECHISTS

MAUREEN MADDEN

Reflections on the Catechism

TWENTY THIRD 23rd
PUBLICATIONS

Contents

About This Series

The *Jump Starts for Catechists* series offers catechists
   quick, hands-on tips for their faith formation sessions.
Each booklet provides practical and classroom-tested
   information, formation, and ideas
   that are valuable for beginning
     as well as experienced catechists.

The books are written by some of
   Twenty-Third Publications' best-selling authors,
     including Gwen Costello, Daniel Connors,
     Sr. Mary Kathleen Glavich, and Alison Berger.
Other books available in this series include
   Discipline Tips, Seasonal Activities, Key Teachings,
   Rites and Rituals, The Early Church, Stories that Teach,
   The Liturgical Year, and *The Prayer Journey.*

Reflections on the Catechism

A valuable, pocket-sized catechist formation tool,
   Reflections on the Catechism combines quotations
   from the *Catechism of the Catholic Church* (CCC)
     with brief, insightful reflections and stories.
The author focuses on articles that are handpicked for catechists
   and their teaching ministry.
Reflections also include thoughtful questions
   and prayers for journaling.
It's inspiring, motivating, and informative!

A Note to Catechists

Thank you for your ministry as a catechist,
   which is an essential ministry in the church.
As a catechist you echo the message of Jesus,
   sharing the good news that has resounded in your heart.
You speak the message both in your words and in your actions.
This booklet was written
   as a way to express gratitude to you
      and to enable you to grow in your ministry.
A quotation from the *Catechism of the Catholic Church*
   begins each section.
Both the quotation and the reflection that follows
   focus on some aspect of catechesis.
The reflection questions and prayers may lead you
   to further insights or to journal writing.
You may choose to read one section each week
   as a way of keeping your focus
   on what is essential in your ministry—
      that is, leading your learners to communion with Jesus.
Again, thank you for the gift you share.
Thank you for echoing the message
   of the good news of Jesus Christ.

Prayer of a Catechist

Catechesis should be permeated with adoration and respect for the name of our Lord Jesus Christ. (CCC 2145)

Lord Jesus Christ,
   let me speak your name in a prayerful whisper,
   knowing that you are near,
   knowing that you hold me close
      as a shepherd holds a sheep.
Lord Jesus Christ,
   let me speak your name in bold proclamation,
   announcing the good news,
      telling all of your saving power.
Lord Jesus Christ,
   let me speak your name with respect,
   with knee bent,
   with head bowed,
   with heart open.
Lord Jesus Christ,
   let me speak your name in adoration,
   filled with gratitude and love,
   filled with wonder and awe,
      as I speak the name that is above all other names.

1.

Union with Christ

Catechesis aims at putting "people…in communion…with Jesus Christ: only he can lead us to the love of the Father in the Spirit and make us share in the life of the Holy Trinity."
(*Catechesi tradendae* [CT] 5 in CCC 426)

"Catechesis aims at putting people
    in communion with Jesus Christ."
When you focus on the essential aspect of catechesis,
    you discover in the apostle Andrew
        an excellent example of the role of a catechist.
For instance, in the Gospel of John,
    Andrew is mentioned three times,
        and each time Andrew leads someone to Jesus.
The gospel tells us that after Andrew meets Jesus:
    "[Andrew] first found his brother Simon and said to him,
        'We have found the Messiah' (which is translated Anointed).
        He brought Simon to Jesus" (1:41–42).
The twelfth chapter of the gospel tells us
    that some Greeks who want to meet Jesus go to Philip.
Philip does not take them directly to Jesus
    but goes first to Andrew.
Andrew and Philip then go together to tell Jesus (12:20–22).

My favorite account of Andrew bringing someone to Christ
   is found in John 6,
      the account of the multiplication of the loaves and fish.

Andrew says to Jesus, "There is a boy here
   who has five barley loaves and two fish" (6:9).
How did Andrew know about the boy's food?
He may have been the type of person
   who was easy to talk to.
He was approachable.
The boy probably told Andrew about his loaves and fish
   because Andrew took the time to listen.

As a catechist, you want to be approachable.
   The learners will know that you are interested in them
      and will listen to what they have to say.
Then, like Andrew, you will be able to bring others to Jesus
   so he can lead them to the "love of the Father in the Spirit"
   (CCC 426).

To Think About

• Which people in your life have been like Andrew, leading you to the Lord?

• What loaves and fish, that is, what gifts do you offer to the Lord?

Prayer

Jesus, may my first goal in teaching the faith always be to lead the learners to you. Everything else—lessons, activities, prayers—are a means you use to help us all grow in communion with you. Bless and guide my efforts; bless all those I teach so we may be open to your Holy Spirit. Amen.

2.

Speaking for Christ

*In catechesis "Christ, the Incarnate Word and Son of God…
is taught—everything else is taught with reference to him—
and it is Christ alone who teaches—anyone else teaches
to the extent that he is Christ's spokesman,
enabling Christ to teach with his lips."* (CT 6 in CCC 427)

"My teaching is not mine but his who sent me" (Jn 7:16).
What an awesome privilege it is to be sent by God!

The Old and New Testaments record numerous examples
    of God sending forth his messengers.
To Moses: "I will send you to Pharaoh
    to bring my people, the Israelites, out of Egypt.
    I will be with you; and this shall be the sign for you
        that it is I who sent you" (Ex 3:10,12).
To Jeremiah: "Before I formed you in the womb I knew you,
    and before you were born I consecrated you;
    I appointed you a prophet to the nations.
    Do not say, 'I am only a boy'…for I am with you" (Jer 1:5, 7–8).
To the apostles: "Go therefore and make disciples of all nations,
    baptizing them in the name of the Father and of the Son
        and of the Holy Sprit, and teaching them to obey
        everything that I have commanded you.

And remember, I am with you always, to the end of the age"
   (Mt 28:19–20).

What an awesome privilege for Moses,
   for Jeremiah and the prophets,
   and for the apostles to be sent by God.
What an overwhelming task, yet what a powerful assurance:
   "I am with you."

You are sent as a catechist, while realizing
   that "it is Christ alone who teaches—
   anyone else teaches to the extent
   that he is Christ's spokesperson,
      enabling Christ to teach with his lips."
You, too, have an awesome role, but you also have
   the Lord's assurance: "I am with you."

To Think About

- When were you first aware of God's call?
- When are you most aware of God's empowering presence in your life?

Prayer

Loving God, thank you for calling me to the ministry of catechesis. Like the prophets and apostles, my privileged mission is to be your spokesperson. In carrying out this overwhelming task, I have your promise: "I am with you." May I recall your presence as I prepare and present lessons on the faith to those I teach. I ask this in Jesus' name. Amen.

3.

The Fullness of Faith

*"Catechesis is an education in the faith of children,
young people, and adults which includes especially the teaching
of Christian doctrine imparted, generally speaking, in an organic
and systematic way, with a view to initiating the hearer into the
fullness of Christian life."* (CT 18 in CCC 5)

As I read this quote from the *Catechism,*
  the phrase "organic and systematic way" stood out.
Each of our lessons is part of a whole.
Each chapter has a place within each unit,
  each unit contributes to the content of the book,
    and each book correlates to the others in the series.
When viewed in their totality, all these components
  help initiate learners into the fullness of Christian life.
You may sometimes be prone to focus
  on each lesson in isolation.
You may fail to see the relationship of one lesson to another
  or the interconnectedness of one theme to another.

From time to time, a myopic view of lessons
  can be corrected by reading the table of contents
  or the scope and sequence chart
    in the teacher's manual.

When you are truly ready to view the whole picture,
    you will also become aware that each lesson
        you prepare and present
        is accepted by God as a gift.
How awesome to think that God uses your gifts
    to help lead your learners to the "fullness of Christian life."

To Think About

- In what ways does your "vision" need to be corrected?

- How often have you paused to look with wonder at the ways God uses your gifts to help your learners?

Prayer

Jesus, our Teacher, as I prepare my lesson each week, give me insight to see it as part of a whole, of your whole plan of salvation. Through catechesis you desire to initiate each person into the fullness of life in you. May I share this desire as I fulfill my role in the church. Amen.

4.

A 2000-Year-Old Ministry

Quite early on, the name catechesis was given to the totality of the church's efforts to make disciples, to help others believe that Jesus is the Son of God so that believing they might have life in his name, and to educate and instruct them in this life, thus building up the body of Christ. (CCC 4; cf CT 1; 2)

The phrase "Quite early on" introduces
    this quote from the *Catechism*.
Through the decades, through the centuries,
    through the two millennia of the church's history,
    the term *catechesis* has been used,
        and catechists have echoed the message of Christ.
It is amazing to think that a message
    proclaimed two thousand years ago
    is still proclaimed today.
That message has incredible impact and power.
To be a catechist who proclaims the word—
    to be part of the church's effort to make disciples
    and to build up the body of Christ—
        calls for perseverance and prayer.

You may be dismayed or even discouraged
    when a lesson is not going exactly as planned:
    when you have repeated the same idea a number of times
        and the students still do not understand;
    when the learners seem bored or distracted;
    when problems and difficulties distract you;
    when one learner's conduct interferes
        with the flow of the lesson.

Instead of being overwhelmed by the difficulties,
    pause and pray.
Ask God to help you realize that your ministry
    is part of the age-old ministry of catechesis.
You will be in awe of the immense power of God
    working through the ages
        in this essential task of the church.

To Think About

- Which catechists have made a difference in your life?
- Which catechists have been role models for you in your ministry?

Prayer

God of mercy, through the ages you built up your church through the work of men and women who responded to your call: make disciples of all nations. When I feel discouraged or inadequate for this task, remind me of those who preceded me in proclaiming your word. May I rely on your immense power and the impact of your message to transform the learners entrusted to me. Amen.

5.

Nurturing Inner Growth

"Catechesis is intimately bound up with the whole of the church's life....Her inner growth and correspondence with God's plan depend essentially on catechesis." (CT 13 in CCC 7)

In our everyday lives certain frequently asked questions
   are rather easy to answer.
Adults often discuss topics such as:
   What kind of car do you drive?

   Where did you go for vacation?

   What team do you think will win the Super Bowl this year?

   How many pounds did you lose on your diet?
Children often discuss questions such as:
   What did you get on your test?

   How old are you?

   Who is your favorite rock star?

   What is your favorite football team?

   What is your favorite video game?
Many of our daily questions can be readily answered
   because the answers are easily measured and assessed.

As catechists you cannot measure
   what you have accomplished with your learners.
A catechist's task is to facilitate "God's plan"
   by nurturing the "inner growth" of the learners.
Only God can measure those results.

To Think About

- Do you become so concerned with measuring the academic progress of your learners that you lose sight of the essential task of catechesis?

- Do you pose questions to yourself and to your learners that can lead to spiritual growth?

Prayer

Jesus, like the sower in your parable, I plant the seed, but it is God who gives the growth. I may not see the inner working of your Spirit in the persons I teach. Give me confidence and trust in God's plan and presence in the essential task of catechesis. Amen.

6.

The Precious Pearl

*Whoever is called to "teach Christ" must first seek "the surpass-
ing worth of knowing Christ Jesus"; he must suffer "the loss of
all things…in order to gain Christ and be found in him," and
"to know him and the power of his resurrection."*
(Phil 3:8–11 in CCC 428)

The words "surpassing worth" remind me of the parable
   Jesus told about the merchant seeking fine pearls.
The man in the parable found one pearl
   that was exceedingly precious.
He sold everything he possessed in order to obtain
   that one priceless pearl.

Often in our materialistic society, the value of possessions
   varies greatly within a short period of time.
Interest rates and stock prices rise and fall.
The value of a house is different this year
   than it was last year or even just a few months ago.
Toys and fads that were popular several months ago
   are discarded as obsolete today.
The items for which we long and work and save
   satisfy us for only a brief period
     before we begin to long for something else.

In the midst of a consumerism that creates expensive items
which inevitably have only a passing value,
people question whether there is anything of lasting value.
The lasting value, the surpassing worth, is to know Jesus.
Only Jesus can fill our deepest longings.

The only priceless treasure is to know Jesus.
And you, as a catechist, can communicate this to your learners
through your words and example.

To Think About

- Are there "treasures" that hinder you from recognizing the surpassing worth of knowing Jesus?

- How do you face the challenge of teaching Christian values to learners raised in a materialistic, consumer society?

Prayer

Lord Jesus, in order to teach others about you, may I share in the mystery of your suffering, death, and resurrection. Only by making you the center of my life will I be able to help those I teach seek you as their priceless treasure. Amen.

7.

Responding to the Call

Those who with God's help have welcomed Christ's call and freely responded to it are urged on by love of Christ to proclaim the Good News everywhere in the world. (CCC 3)

Do you have caller ID on your telephone?
Do you let your answering machine pick up to see who is calling
    before you decide whether or not you want to talk?
Do you screen calls so frequently that your family and friends
    begin their message by saying, "I know you're there.
        Please pick up the phone!"?

Are you selective in listening to the call of Christ?
    The apostles left all behind to respond to Jesus' call.
Simon and Andrew, James and John left their families
    and their fishing boats to become disciples.
Matthew walked away from his tax collector's table
    and from his way of life to follow the Lord.
Responding to Christ's call means making decisions
    that give evidence of your identity as Jesus' followers.
Responding to Christ's call means
    making the commitment each day
        to choose the values of Jesus rather than the values
        often promoted by society and by the media.

Responding to Christ's call means being
   "urged on by the love of Christ"
   until people see that love
      reflected in your words and actions.

To Think About

- Which of your actions clearly reveal that you are "urged on by the love of Christ"?

- In what specific ways have you put into practice the challenging words of the gospel?

Prayer

Loving God, in my daily decisions, I hear your voice urging me to act as your Son Jesus would. This means renewing my commitment to choose the values of Jesus. In so doing, may I teach my learners how to love as Jesus did. Amen.

8.

The "Yes" of Faith

From the loving knowledge of Christ springs the desire to proclaim him, to "evangelize," and to lead others to the "yes" of faith in Jesus Christ. (CCC 429)

A man named Steve practiced for months
   walking across a tightrope
      that he had stretched across his backyard.
The tightrope was raised only a few feet off the ground
   but Steve gave all of his attention to his practice
      just as if the rope were actually suspended
      at a dangerous height.
Next, he began walking across it pushing a wheelbarrow.
Then, he added bricks to the wheelbarrow.

Steve's neighbor, Jesse, had observed him for months,
   and he finally decided to question Steve.
Steve told him that he intended to walk across a tightrope
   that was stretched across Niagara Falls.
Steve asked Jesse, "Do you think I can do it?"
Jesse assured him that he had faith in his ability.

Again and again, Steve demanded assurances
   of Jesse's confidence.

Again and again Jesse said that he believed in his neighbor.
Finally, Steve asked how much Jesse weighed.
When Jesse told him that he weighed 160 pounds,
    Steve said, "I have been pushing 160 pounds of bricks
        in my wheelbarrow.
If you truly have faith in me,
    you will get in the wheelbarrow
        when I cross Niagara Falls."

The "yes" of faith is more than a verbal affirmation.
    The "yes" of faith demands an active response.
It means committing your life to Christ,
    placing your full confidence in him.
Do you trust in his help
    when you encounter problems in your ministry?
Think of the example of Mary
    who was asked to be the mother of God's son.
You can use her example
    and that of the saints
        to talk about the "yes" of faith.

To Think About

- Jesus asks, "Do you believe?" What is your response?
- How do your actions witness to your beliefs?

Prayer

Jesus, the "yes" you ask of your followers is one that expresses itself in deeds, not words alone. Your mother, Mary, is my model of that "yes." May my desire to follow you lead those I teach to express their "yes" of faith in you. Amen.

9.

The Family's Role

Family catechesis precedes, accompanies, and enriches other forms of instruction in the faith. Parents have the mission of teaching their children to pray and to discover their vocation as children of God. (CCC 2226)

The primary responsibility
for educating a child or teen in the faith
belongs to the parents.
It is their right and their privilege.
As a catechist you assist the family in this task.

The catechesis that takes place in the home
is most often occasional,
while the catechesis carried out
in the religious education program
is more systematic.
To say that catechesis in the home is occasional
does not mean that it takes place
only occasionally or infrequently.
Rather, the family uses the occasions
that arise as part of daily events in the home
to instruct their children and teens.

For example, if a child has an argument with a sister or brother,
the parents correct the behavior.
But they usually do not ask the child
which of the commandments has been broken.

Your role as catechist is to help the learner organize and name
what he or she has learned in the family.
You can assist the family by helping the child
develop a religious vocabulary
and attain a certain core of knowledge of the faith.
Parents and catechists work hand in hand.
Always, "family catechesis precedes, accompanies,
and enriches" the instruction provided
in the religious education program.

To Think About

- Do you recognize that you are a partner to the parents in the religious education of their children?

- In what concrete ways do you assist the parents, recognizing that theirs is the primary role?

Prayer

Loving God, I recognize the primary role of the family in the religious education of their children. Guide me in finding ways to support them and partner with them in their vital task of helping one another grow in faith. Amen.

10.

Choosing Life

The way of Christ "leads to life"; a contrary way "leads to destruction." The gospel parable of the two ways remains ever present in the catechesis of the church; it shows the importance of moral decisions for our salvation. "There are two ways, the one of life, the other of death"; but between the two, there is a great difference. (Mt 7:13; Dt 30:15–20 in CCC 1696)

In the book of Deuteronomy,
    Moses challenges the Israelites to make a decision:
    "See, I have set before you today life and prosperity,
        death and adversity.
    If you obey the commandments of the Lord your God
        that I am commanding you today,
        by loving the Lord your God,
        walking in his ways, and observing his commandments....
    Choose life so that you and your descendants may live"
        (30:15–16,19).

The choice seems an easy one.
Who would not choose life?
Yet many in our world today have chosen the other way.
Pope John Paul II often spoke
    of the "culture of death" that envelops us.

Violence and abuse, wars and destruction,
  greed and envy; all exist and spread.
We cannot ignore the reality.
Even more disturbing is the fact
  that the media portrays some aspects of the culture of death
    as ways to achieve success.

Moses challenged the people to "choose life and prosperity."
In so many instances today, what is touted as success
  leads to death rather than life.
How important and yet how difficult is your responsibility
  to teach children the importance
    of making good moral decisions.
The way of Christ leads to life, for he told us,
"I came that they may have life, and have it abundantly" (Jn 10:10).

To Think About

• What messages promoted in the media do you find most
destructive?

• In what ways have you been tempted to define "success"
according to the media instead of according to the gospel?

Prayer

*Jesus, when I follow you, I choose the way of life. Yet as a catechist,
I am surrounded by examples of another way—that of death and
destruction. May I be your instrument in teaching learners the
importance of making good moral decisions, of choosing your way,
the way of life. Amen.*

11.

The Joy and the Challenge

*Catechesis has to reveal in all clarity the joy and the demands
of the way of Christ.* (CCC 1697; cf CT 29)

The apostles Peter, James, and John were with Jesus
    when he was transfigured.
They saw Jesus in glory as he spoke with Moses and Elijah.
The apostles reacted the way we probably would have.
They wanted to capture that moment in time.
Peter said, "Rabbi, it is good for us to be here;
    let us make three dwellings,
        one for you, one for Moses, and one for Elijah" (Mk 9:5).
But Jesus led the apostles down the mountain.
Instead of focusing on the glorious vision
    that had given his disciples immense joy,
Jesus foretold his suffering and death.

Peter, James, and John—
    and each of us—
    must be prepared to embrace
        both the joys and the sorrows of life.

As a catechist, you seek to be a joyful messenger
   of the good news.
But it is also essential to present the demands of the gospel.
When the apostles saw Jesus transfigured,
   they heard the Father's voice from heaven say:
   "This is my Son, the Beloved; listen to him!" (Mk 9:7).
Each of us strives to recognize Jesus, the Son of God
   and listen to his words.
We listen for the messages that challenge
   as well as those that comfort.

As a catechist you want to help your learners to listen to Jesus.
You will teach in such a way that you "reveal in all clarity
   the joy and the demands of the way of Christ."

To Think About

- Which words of the gospel do you find the most comforting?

- Which words of the gospel do you find the most challenging?

Prayer

Jesus, beloved Son of the Father, you have taught us that living your Word entails joy as well as demands. May I have the courage to present to those I teach the messages of the gospel that challenge as well as those that comfort. I ask this through the intercession of Mary, your mother. Amen.

12.

The Aspects of Catechesis

Catechesis for the "newness of life" in Christ should be: a catechesis of the Holy Spirit; a catechesis of grace; a catechesis of the beatitudes; a catechesis of sin and forgiveness; a catechesis of the human virtues; a catechesis of the Christian virtues of faith, hope, and charity; a catechesis of the twofold commandment of charity; and an ecclesial catechesis. (CCC 1697)

The *Catechism of the Catholic Church* discusses in detail
    each of the aspects of catechesis listed above.
The texts used in religious education programs
    also present each of these themes
        because each is an essential component of our faith.
Not all the themes are covered at each grade level,
    but they are presented in a sequential
    and age-appropriate manner.

There is such richness in our Catholic faith.
All too often, we may focus on the topic
    that is most familiar to us
    or the one that is our favorite.

We miss so much when we limit ourselves
    to just a small portion of our tradition.

As you approach a lesson in the text, take the time
    to reflect on the theme
    and its meaning in your life.
Deepen your understanding and appreciation
    of its mystery.
Then you will be better able to lead your learners
    on the path of discipleship.

As you teach each lesson, be well aware
    of the core content of the chapter,
        and be sure to emphasize and repeat it.
Help the learners grasp the meaning.
Help each to grow in the different aspects of our faith
    as they embrace more fully the "newness of life in Christ."

To Think About

- Which of the themes listed in the *Catechism* is your favorite to teach?

- In which area are you most in need of growth?

Prayer

Loving God, you have revealed your very self to us, especially in Jesus, your son. The richness of the faith we express requires a life-long study. May I grow daily in my understanding of this faith so I can present each aspect as fully as possible to those I teach. I ask this in Jesus' name. Amen.

13.

The Action of the Spirit

Catechesis should be a catechesis of the Holy Spirit, the interior Master of life according to Christ, a gentle guest and friend who inspires, guides, corrects, and strengthens this life. (CCC 1697)

Prior to their confirmation,
   young learners spend time
      in prayer, in study, and in service.
During each practice session for the celebration,
   the youth are instructed to say with conviction
   the phrase "I do!" as the bishop asks them,
      "Do you believe in God the Father Almighty...?
      Do you believe in Jesus Christ...?
      Do you believe in the Holy Spirit...?"

When the candidates stand before the bishop,
   the priests, their parents, their sponsors,
   and the entire congregation,
      they profess their faith with prayerfulness.
The bishop asked, "Do you believe in the Holy Spirit,
   the Lord, the giver of life,

who came upon the apostles at Pentecost
and today is given to you sacramentally in confirmation?"
Their "I do" expresses their commitment to the faith.
What a wonderful and awesome gift!
The Holy Spirit does not act in our lives
only at baptism and confirmation.
Through the virtues and gifts of the Spirit
we are able to grow in love for God.

You can lead your learners to a fuller knowledge and experience
of the action of the Spirit in their lives.
Share with them your own experience,
pray with them,
encourage them to become aware of the work of the Spirit,
not only in the sacraments, but in their good works,
in nature, in all God's gifts.

To Think About

• Is your faith professed in bold proclamations as well as in hushed tones filled with wonder and awe?

• Are you open to the gifts of the Spirit, the Lord, the giver of life?

Prayer

Holy Spirit, giver of life, fill my mind and heart with your grace. May I be open to your gifts so you may speak through me as I proclaim God's word to those I teach. I ask this in Jesus' name. Amen.

14.

The Gift of Grace

Catechesis should be a catechesis of grace, for it is by grace that we are saved and again it is by grace that our works can bear fruit for eternal life. (CCC 1697)

A number of years ago
   I was holding a contest in my religious education program
   to encourage the learners
      to develop their religious vocabulary.
Each of the questions in the contest was a definition
   from the glossary in their religion texts.
One of the words in the first-grade text was "grace."
   It seemed an excellent choice for learners at each grade level.
Surprisingly, while most of the first graders
   answered that question correctly,
      the majority of the fourth and fifth graders
      could not identify "grace."

The *Catechism* defines grace as
   "a participation in the life of God."
The wording in our first-grade text was
   "God's own life and love in us."
Perhaps the fourth and fifth graders had forgotten
   what they learned in the first grade.

Or perhaps they thought that the correct definition of grace
  was too good to be true.
How easy it is for us to recite a definition.
How readily we acknowledge
  that we receive the gift of grace at baptism.
I wonder how often—
  or how infrequently—
  we pause to marvel
    at the words we are speaking.
Grace is a participation in God's own life;
  it is too good to be true.
Yet it is true!

To Think About

- What does the word "grace" mean to you?

- On a practical level, how does grace touch the daily life of
you and your learners?

Prayer

*God of light and life, we receive your gift of grace at baptism. Yet
how often grace remains only a word, a definition, in our daily
lives. May my wonder and appreciation of this gift grow daily. And
may I communicate this attitude and the reality of grace to those I
teach. In Jesus' name. Amen.*

15.

The Promise
of the Beatitudes

Catechesis should be a catechesis of the beatitudes,
for the way of Christ is summed up in the beatitudes,
the only path that leads to the eternal beatitude
for which the human heart longs. (CCC 1697)

To people in search of happiness
   and people in search of a home,
      God gives an answer.
In the book of Genesis,
   God promised to lead Abraham and his wife, Sarah,
   to a new land in which they and their descendants
      would dwell.
God's assurance to Abraham was: "I will bless you…
   so that you will be a blessing" (Gn 12:2).

In the New Testament, Jesus promises us an eternal dwelling.
Instead of the possession of a territory,
   Jesus promises the kingdom of heaven.
Again, words of blessing are spoken.
Jesus assures us:
   "Blessed are the poor in spirit…

Blessed are those who mourn...

Blessed are the meek...

Blessed are those who hunger and thirst for righteousness...

Blessed are the merciful...

Blessed are the pure in heart...

Blessed are the peacemakers...

Blessed are those who are persecuted for righteousness' sake...

Blessed are you when people revile you and persecute you..."

(Mt 5:3–12)

The *Catechism* describes the beatitudes
  as paradoxical promises that sustain hope
    in the midst of tribulation.
The beatitudes express the vocation of the faithful.
The beatitudes shed light on the actions and the attitudes
  characteristic of the Christian life (CCC 1716).

To Think About

- Which beatitude best describes you?

- How do you present the beatitudes to your learners?

Prayer

Jesus, our Teacher, in the beatitudes you describe the path to eternal happiness. The beatitudes are promises that offer hope. Show me how to share this hope by teaching my learners how to practice the beatitudes in their daily lives. Amen.

16.

Need for Forgiveness

*Catechesis should be a catechesis of sin and forgiveness,
for unless a person acknowledges that he is a sinner, he cannot
know the truth about himself, which is a condition for acting
justly; and without the offer of forgiveness he would not
be able to bear this truth.* (CCC 1697)

Late in the evening,
   as Holy Thursday became Good Friday,
   Peter and Judas each turned away from their Lord.
Both of these apostles betrayed the one who loved them.
Judas sold Jesus for thirty pieces of silver.
Peter denied that he was an apostle
   and denied that he even knew Jesus.
Similar actions, yet what a great difference
   in the reaction of the two men.
Judas despaired and killed himself.
Peter wept and repented.
He trusted that Jesus, who had spoken so often of forgiveness,
   would forgive even this sin.

During the Passover meal,
   Jesus took the cup of wine in his hands
   and said, "Take this, all of you, and drink from it:

this is the cup of my blood,
the blood of the new and everlasting covenant.
It will be shed for you and for all
so that sins may be forgiven."
Peter trusted the words Jesus had spoken.
He believed.

When we are aware of our sins and conscious of our failings,
we are also aware of Jesus' mercy,
and that makes all the difference.
Each time we approach the sacrament of reconciliation,
we hear the words that assure us of God's mercy.

To Think About

- Do you believe and trust in God's mercy?
- How often do you celebrate the sacrament of reconciliation?
- How do your words and actions invite your learners to celebrate God's mercy in the sacrament of reconciliation?

Prayer

God of mercy, acknowledging that we are sinners helps us know the truth about ourselves. Believing in your forgiveness enables us to accept the truth. In teaching others about sin and forgiveness, may I always stress your merciful love, shown in the sacrament of reconciliation. Amen.

17.

Growth in Virtue

*Catechesis should be a catechesis of the human virtues
which causes one to grasp the beauty and attraction
of right dispositions towards goodness; a catechesis
of the Christian virtues of faith, hope, and charity,
generously inspired by the example of the saints.* (CCC 1697)

How would you describe yourself?
Most often, the first description we give
   of ourselves or of others
    is a list of physical characteristics.
Go beyond the external.
Look within.
Instead of external characteristics,
   consider your internal character.
How would you describe yourself?
We sometimes have the tendency
   to focus on the negative.
We examine imperfections and flaws
   and fail to see the positive.

Saint Paul counsels the Philippians: "Whatever is true,
   whatever is honorable, whatever is just, whatever is pure,
   whatever is pleasing, whatever is commendable,

if there is any excellence
   and if there is anything worthy of praise,
   think about these things" (Phil 4:8).
Take time to think about virtues
   and to recognize the virtues you live,
      especially those that help you in your calling as catechist.
Pray for God's help to grow in virtue.
Offer thanks to God
   for the gifts of faith, hope, and love.

In your ministry as a catechist,
   strive to recognize and affirm
      the good in your learners.
Negative comments and sarcastic remarks
   can affect their self-image.
Do your best to affirm
   the good attitudes, habits, and behaviors
      of the learners you teach.

To Think About

- In what practical ways are your faith and hope in evidence?
- In what ways are your acts of charity a response to the love God bestows upon you?

Prayer

Jesus, in the gospels we find so many examples of virtue: your kindness, respect for others, forgiveness, and more. Show me how to point out these virtues in a concrete way to those I teach. Amen.

18.

The Great Commandments

Catechesis should be a catechesis of the twofold commandment of charity set forth in the Decalogue. (CCC 1697)

A legend told about Saint John,
   known as the beloved apostle,
   says that at the end of his long life
   many of his closest friends
      would gather around to be instructed by him.
They wanted to learn all they could from this man
   who had walked with Jesus,
   who had witnessed his miracles,
   who had stood beneath the cross,
   and who had witnessed the resurrection.
Day after day, the group listened.
Yet no matter what the topic
   and no matter what the question,
      John always spoke about love.
Finally one of the listeners asked,
   "John, why is it that you always speak about love?"
John replied, "Love is all there is."

The legend may not be true
    but it reflects much of what is contained
    in the First Letter of John.
"Beloved, let us love one another,
    because love is from God;
    everyone who loves is born of God
    and knows God....God is love" (1 Jn 4:7–8).

John had learned from Jesus' words
    and from Jesus' life of love.
He knew the importance of the commandment of love,
    given in the Old Testament and confirmed by Jesus:
    "You shall love the Lord your God with all your heart,
        and with all your soul, and with all your mind.
    You shall love your neighbor as yourself" (Mt 22:37, 39).

To Think About

- Which of your actions show most concretely your love for God?
- Which of your actions show your love of neighbor?

Prayer

Jesus, through example and word you taught us love for God and for one another. These two great commandments are at the heart of all the others. Help me show those I teach how to apply these commandments to their daily lives. Amen.

19.

Ministers of the Church

Catechesis should be an ecclesial catechesis, for it is through the manifold exchanges of spiritual goods in the community of saints that Christian life can grow, develop, and be communicated. (CCC 1697)

As you teach about the church, you also minister
    as members of the church.
You are not alone in your ministry.
Catechesis should be an ecclesial catechesis.
You are commissioned during the celebration of Mass,
    called forth from the assembly
    and blessed for your ministry
        to teach the faith of the church.

Throughout the year,
    the pastor, the parish staff, and members of the parish
        enfold you in prayer.
Throughout your lives, the patron saints of the catechists
    intercede for you in heaven.
Consider the long, unbroken line of catechists
    who have served throughout the history of the church.

Consider the holy men and women who have gone before you
　　as teachers and preachers.
Consider the martyrs who have shed their blood
　　as members of this church to which you belong.
Think about the learners in your group who may one day
　　stand before another group as their catechist.

For now they are the learners
　　who sit in your class
　　　　(or are restless),
　　who excel in your class
　　　　(or who yawn in your class),
　　who always have their lessons prepared
　　　　(or who never have their books),
　　who look with eyes of wonder
　　　　(or who look out the window).
Think of the learners who,
　　from time to time remember you,
　　　　as they pray, "God bless our catechist."

To Think About

- How is your ministry part of the ministry of the church?
- Was there one particular catechist who had a special impact on your life of faith?

Prayer

Loving God, in the Body of Christ we are joined to the communion of saints in heaven and on earth. May what we teach always be in accord with the faith shared by the church. Amen.

20.

Liturgy and Catechesis

*Catechesis is intrinsically linked with the whole of liturgical
and sacramental activity, for it is in the sacraments,
especially in the Eucharist, that Christ Jesus works in fullness
for the transformation of people.* (CT 23 in CCC 1074)

A retreat was being given in a nearby parish.
In attendance were nearly thirty faith-filled people
    who had chosen to spend their entire weekend
        in reflection and prayer.
Most of the retreatants were among
    the most active in the parish.
Many of them attended daily Mass.

The retreatants were gathered in the school building
    to listen to a talk by one of the priests of the parish.
As the presentation reached its conclusion,
    the priest gave directions
        for the time of quiet reflection that would follow.
He suggested that each retreatant reflect on one sentence
    from the Eucharistic Prayer.

Each person should select his or her favorite sentence,
  one that had particular meaning.

As the talk concluded, the thirty adults walked
  from the school to the church.
Instead of beginning their time of reflection,
  each person hurried to find a missalette
    in order to read the Eucharistic Prayer.
None of them was able to identify a sentence
  without referring to the missalette.
How often had each retreatant attended Mass?

How often have *you* attended Mass?
How often, perhaps, have you been distracted
  instead of focused on the prayers?
How often have you appreciated
  the power, beauty, and meaning of the prayers?

To Think About

- What is your favorite sentence in the Eucharistic Prayer?

- In what ways can you lead your learners to a better appreciation of the liturgy?

Prayer

God of love, the church celebrates the paschal mystery of your son at every liturgy. The liturgy is therefore a wonderful catechesis for each of us, both catechists and learners. May I enrich my teaching with the liturgy in specific ways, so my learners will acquire a deeper knowledge and experience of both. Amen.

21.

Prayer

Catechesis is a time for the discernment and education of popular piety. The memorization of basic prayers offers an essential support to the life of prayer, but it is important to help learners savor their meaning. (CCC 2688)

Have you ever taken young children
    to a fancy restaurant for a gourmet meal?
If your answer is yes, you probably would agree
    that most young children do not understand
        how to "savor" a good meal.
The fast food generation pays more attention
    to the toy in the kid's meal
        than to the meal itself.

It is also the case
    that young children do not usually "savor"
        the meaning of prayers.
In fact, for the very young,
    it is sometimes an accomplishment
    to learn which shoulder to touch first
        when making the Sign of the Cross.
Young children, though, have a keen awareness
    that prayer is a conversation with God.

They sometimes have a reverence
   that adults cannot easily attain.
As children grow older and learn their prayers,
   this conversation with God
      might become a matter of routine.
One of your significant tasks as a catechist
   is to invite the learners to pray with reverence
   and with a sense of awe for the nearness
      of God who loves us.

A good way for you to instruct the learners
   is by being a role model in prayer.
The catechist who prays with and for the learners,
   the catechist who prays with reverence,
   the catechist whose prayer comes from the heart
      as well as from the head,
   the catechist who truly "savors" the meaning of prayer
      will be an effective model for his or her learners.

To Think About

- What is your favorite prayer?
- When did you first learn to pray?
- When have you experienced the power of prayer?

Prayer

Holy God, you are always with us, even when we are not present to you. Teach me to love you more and more and entrust my life to you, so I may be a model of prayer for those I teach. Amen.

22.

Meditating on God's Word

*The catechesis of children, young people, and adults aims
at teaching them to meditate on the word of God in personal
prayer, practicing it in liturgical prayer, and internalizing it at
all times in order to bear fruit in a new life.* (CCC 2688)

The story is told of an elderly man who lived by himself
    about a mile from a small town.
The people of the town were poor and uneducated.
The man, who was able to read,
    came to the town each day.
He sat beside a tall tree,
    gathered the children around him,
    and read to them from the Bible.
The children especially loved to hear the gospel accounts
    of Jesus' miracles and teaching.
Gradually, however, the man began to have difficulty
    focusing on the printed words.
He visited the doctor, who examined him
    and then shared the distressing news.
The man's vision was deteriorating rapidly
    and there was nothing that could be done to correct it.

He would soon be blind.
During the next days and weeks,
    the man did not come to the town.
The townspeople were worried about him,
    thinking he must be very depressed.
At their urging,
    the doctor went to visit the man.
The doctor found him reading the Bible
    and could see that he was at peace
        and even seemed happy.
He told the doctor that, for as long as he could,
    he would read and reread passages of the Bible,
        committing them to memory.
Then, when he could no longer see,
    he would still be able to share with the children
        the gospel, now printed on his heart.

The elderly man in the story offers an inspiring example
    of meditation on the word of God.
To know the gospel so well
    that it is printed on your heart
    is a goal to which each catechist
        would want to aspire.

To Think About

- How often do you meditate on the word of God?

- Do you treasure God's word in your heart as Mary did?

Prayer

Jesus, your words are the pearls of wisdom that we seek. May I treasure them in my heart, so I may teach my learners to do the same. Amen.

23.

The Way, the Truth, and the Life

The first and last point of reference of catechesis will always be Jesus Christ himself, who is "the way, and the truth, and the life" (Jn 14:6). By looking to him in faith Christ's faithful can hope that he himself fulfills his promises in them, and, by loving him with the same love with which he has loved them, they may perform works in keeping with their dignity. (CCC 1698)

Jesus is the Alpha and the Omega,
   the first and the last.
Jesus is the way, the truth, and the life.
When your journey seems to be a series of
   detours with confusing road signs,
     highways where you travel at high speed
      without ever approaching your destination,
   choices to make about which way to follow,
   take assurance in the knowledge
     that Jesus is the Way.

When you are confronted with
   half-truths and blatant lies,
     misquoted and misleading statements,

decisions to make as to what to believe,
take courage in the assurance that Jesus is the Truth.

When you encounter a culture
that promotes destructive behaviors
that degrades and demeans the value of life,
that challenges you to live out the catechesis of the liturgy,
draw strength from the conviction that Jesus is the Life.

Jesus is the Alpha and the Omega,
the first and the last.
Follow his way,
speak his truth,
and share in his life
through prayer and the celebration of the sacraments.

To Think About

• When and how have you chosen to follow Jesus the Way instead of following "the crowd"?

• Have you been faithful in speaking the truth that leads to life?

Prayer

Jesus, you are our way, truth, and life. Show me the path to follow, let your truth take root in my mind and heart, and let the abundant life you give us through the sacraments be the living water that quenches our thirst. Amen.